The Rainy Season Diaries

To Gordon –

I hope you enjoy
these poem-stories!

:)

[signature]
Nov, 2013
Istanbul

The Rainy Season Diaries

Jennifer A. Reimer

A ClearSound Book from QUALE PRESS

Untitled selections from this manuscript have appeared in the *Denver Quarterly, The Berkeley Poetry Review, The Chaffey Review, 580 Split, Tinfish, Puerto del Sol, Zoland, Weave Magazine,* and *14 Hills.*

Cover image (untitled paper collage) and design by Jason Buchholz

ISBN: 978-1-935835-09-7
LCCN: 2013943370

A ClearSound Book from Quale Press
www.quale.com

for Alfred

Even the heat has left our house. Words unwrapped themselves from silence. You ask me: what is the rate of occurrence? You ask me: how are you spent? But we are engaged in the practice of survival—prisoners in a world that disappears again. I traced your scars even though they have become perfectly soundless. Closer to what can be saved. Now, I can say this. I can say this because you are not here, yet the gate trembles and I think you must be.

We fall asleep on a fault zone. Where surface traces mistake wind for hair, voice for hunger. Down where motion originates, we find clean fractures and the gentle dip and sway of bedrock. We are plates, sliding past each other: the intersection of earth with artery. You and I always apologize before going to bed. We rarely argue. Every night, you place a glass of water on the nightstand that you never drink. In the morning, a thin layer of dust has settled on the surface.

Say my hair is a rope of ashes and wax. In the wind, we become time travelers, bridging the gaps between the decades we knew and the decade we know. I mistake your limbs for sudden distance. What becomes my entire universe: your taste, your exhale, and all the words we forget passing below our house and out toward the empty tide.

From the interior the scarline cuts us. We cover corners with what is missing. We have no map of our countries, only the distant rumble of stone, the cracked and heated earth. Once our continents were roped like a bridge and we fought the still earth. Now distance advances according to our own logic. We have turned off the music to listen to our voices on the phone. In the long pause before a moment of sudden movement, we are homelands, briefly splitting.

We said no place was a place until history happened. Even from here we sense opposites: logic and water. Traces of stories that were not our own. And still we scratched away. A notch in the wood for every day of departure. There was a time when we talked about books, the distant periphery, and we wrung the sweat from the sheets and began again. We said words weren't words—bits of flesh and prose—until you touched me. Your hands in my mouth or your tongue against my teeth.

A list of useful objects: stones, wood, bones, shells. All the disappearing things. We watch the walls where a spider weaves. We move without noise. Do you believe in accidents? Recognize me by my ghosts. I am transparent now, immaterial. Yes, I say, we have plundered and forgotten. You ask me to measure the distant roar of water from the stolen. A golden net for casting. An amber light for a remote sea. Ask me where the lines meet. Ask me.

This emptiness comes from regressing light, where our hunger fills the formal topography of maps. Once we drew longitudes and latitudes in recognizable colors. We invented corresponding stories for sets of numbers. You called 165/15 home. 105/20: fish made of gold. 45/45: the perfect bowl of noodles. And when our bellies were full, we smashed all the china and laughed. Now we begin to count the silverware after dinner parties. Five bottles of wine and three broken glasses. Until our rooms reveal only what can be numbered, collected. What we will pack.

In the middle of all this architecture you are leaving. I will measure what's left by packing suitcases. Not everything will be recorded. Your leaving, for instance, goes unremarked by air and dust, our weary household gods. This is what happens when you leave: I open a book. I make the bed. On the appointed day, I stay indoors. I'm at the window, to answer to my name should you call it. I told you to be visible but that was not a permission, not a mask.

When you hang up you always say—. An awareness of something that needs preserving. We are collecting stories and dust. Today I found ants in the kitchen again. A pause for breath. A dirty window.

It has been raining for so long. We can no longer tell what came in with the rain or what was a memory. The door will no longer shut. I have learned on my own how to ride the monsoon winds, trade fish for bone, a word for a wing. You say my hands are never so transparent that their touch becomes unnecessary. Alone in the afternoon, I wash the walls and polish the floors. Our daily rituals embed such tiny scratches. You create spaces where dust refuses.

Many things have entered. A pool of rainwater. A line of ants. Old names. We are growing gills, breathing. Here we can shout at the top of our voices and have no need for veiled expressions. And while they are destroyed, something can be constructed—windows become whispers and my tongue refuses to dissolve.

When it rains there is more rain and only the points of difference: the shadows our mouths make against each other. Geological time speeds up. I repeat these words to myself: *Dios te salve, María. Llena eres de gracia: El Señor es contigo. Bendita tú eres entre todas las mujeres. Y bendito es el fruto de tu vientre: Jesús. Santa María, Madre de Dios, ruega por nosotros pecadores, ahora y en la hora de nuestra muerte.* Amen. Yes, there are rules. And even though we have been trained for constant motion, we cannot escape our quickening breath, the faster pulse. When we braid flowers into hair, we are plaiting a desperate desire to never leave.

Sunlight became a single and simple moment. Yes, there were doubts at times. But we were moving, the day was hot, and no one thought about consolation. Such small murders, such vast dinner tables. What explains the greater frequency. Between the layers of skin and sun, all the exotic palettes of conquest. The rain is also there. What evaporates into the fold, what pale salts.

Into crest and trench a rule of separation. Do you know how the redwoods smell when it's been raining or how the tiny lights flicker against my naked skin when I'm awake? I want to erase everything beyond faith, beyond fire. Where even an exceedingly normal day gets the angles right and the lines crossed. This is something you never knew: how to breathe deeply enough to conjure the scent of my arousal from the thinning air. Your rage burrowed into the wind.

I pick up the seashells in the bathroom and hold them to my ear. You said it's bad luck to bring seashells into the house, past your marble floors, mosaic tiles and those meticulously carved doors. You said we have no room for coconut palms or other sea words. I thought it was bad luck when you didn't know *crustacean* and *sea star* (not *starfish*). You didn't know how to peel an orange.

This is a lesson that I should not forget. After all, where is a bucket of water to be raised if not from the ground? What was sudden, drying dirt. Rain buried seeds. No, you said, it was birds. An accident of nesting. More than once we have found our laundry in the trees. A feather in the hall. Every night we say we are too tired. Rain breaking surfaces. We sleep on opposite sides, dream of petaled light.

We become time, spent and lost, the damp and throbbing intervals. The arousals, the orgasms, the reading lists. I am practicing words and place names: *honu fanihi talaya tano tasi.* You say these things should not be repeated. You say nothing should be perfect while I summon the wandering spells or mix the sleeping potions. Secrets are prayer books and spice jars. *Kamyo hineksa.* As if we could wager a name for a sunny day, a good night's sleep, and the visible relief of approaching land.

We have neglected our everyday oracles. Someone has swept the salt from beneath the bed. We now define success as the careful maintenance of order. We do not hang crosses above doors anymore. You are comfortably eating *helado de coco* while the ledge crumbles. All I see: a sunken floodplain: absence and leaf. You would open me. The things you tell me you want to see through me: church spires, a desert, a pair of something. There I am waged; there I am skinned.

In hurricane season time is a unifying coordinate. What strikes water and wind are trees and glass. You mention the ancient, the uneven, and feminine. How damage alters the terms of our trades. We argue over rice. The best symbol of—. In the picture, you lean against the banyan tree. But the roots have spoilt the light. *Breadfruit, star fruit, carambola, guava.* I want to love a place we can call paradise, a vanishing prayer for everything we fail to protect.

Today the lavender is blooming. She makes lists to pass the time: Things That Begin to Disappear Slowly Over Time Until One Day They Are Gone. Things I Take. Things in Need of Constant Attention. It was raining and she remembered a dream she had in which it rained for so long that the house began to fall apart. She laughed because it seemed to her that the whole world was not ending, but that it had never existed in the first place. When she woke, the sun was shining. Things Which Begin to Dim Upon Waking. She has collected enough fruit to make preserves but when she went to the kitchen the water wouldn't boil. Strange Things. She found $20 in the pocket of your pants—the ones you left on the chair. She didn't put it on top of the dresser where you keep your watch and spare change. Instead, she put it in her pocket. Tomorrow, she will walk to the store and buy a piece of chocolate.

This restoration of order seemed to work. But the end of hostilities demanded new maps. Of places where we bargained our vanished certitude and all those things that made you want me to want you so close. We pressed ourselves between the sheets and learned that no system is irreversible. We learned hope for an endless accumulation. Which is the most we can ever expect.

A practice of dividing. Cut away from bone, away from flesh. What occupies the remainder? Caution is not enough but it slips in between the sheets. Once I mapped lines into our skin. We said *lick*. We said *slash*. Now lines are not lines, now space is not. A cleaving thing, a reckless thing. A day's length of sun passes over this house like some kind of apparition. Slowly and almost perfect.

At night, the rush and suck becomes a crumbling continent. Our problem is how to turn translations into dinner, a well-ordered household, and meaningful conversation. We come closer to the moment when memories become myths, bedtime stories with no one listening. How long until we become the monsters sleeping beneath the bed.

We will not cross those latitudes of picture books and other dark rooms. We will not seek the clinging parameters of lost light. It is no longer sufficient to say someday the roads will clear, someday we'll unearth truth. Otherwise, there is starvation. Phone calls and plane rides. Missed messages. Somewhere along the way, our appetite changes. We press and slide, sink slick skin into our mouths or travel over fingers, but before the deep, the salty, the layered, we find our sweat has already vanished.

We are surrendered by ghosts. The wild coast still a place for smugglers and other mercenaries. At night we hear the cocaine planes, but we have stopped praying. Our dead do not appear on surfaces: they are traces of dust. Listen: they are whispering their brief exorcisms. Don't tell me about drums in the forest. The walls of our house are beating and we are within them.

In moments before sleep we enter each other. An ancient instinct toward nest and blood, this one exquisite gesture blesses our household objects: a pillow, a page, a white horizon. Incantations: Come closer, come nearer. I can taste myself in your mouth, fresh water and salt. In what tongue (say whole, say winged). Say a song burns.

We have partial hints, indications left on glass that we have finally forgotten our ancient charms and now the magic is ruined. We are left with sticky pots and the disapproving gaze of the cat. Desire drowned in swamps. I say that it's all right as long as the house is clean. On the other side, we disappear into stories. We are witnesses to the wayward and the frightening and yet we cannot bear to look closer.

Our bodies wear out all attempts at geometry. Here an effective reading begins to get out of hand. Plot lines encircle us until we are bound to our intersections. A series of experiments and tactical interventions in longing. What would it take to forget camouflage? In the meantime, we approach mythology with a certain apprehension. Dreams of corridors are our labyrinths.

You have been betrayed by stories. You say this house will never be made of gingerbread. It does not appear to fall apart as the result of huffing and puffing. Wrongly imagining knight errantry was compatible with society, we have converted the poet into a wage laborer. Magic beans are not, if you recall, something we can buy around here. And there are rules about wishing for more wishes. Only the mirror knows the price of transformation. A pot of boiling water. A cat curling into sun.

An open atlas reminds us of our rootlessness. We bend pages: all places cannot be ruined. We trace the gold embossing and understand the charms of nostalgia. You call me by pet names. You say *so much muchness* with the most peculiar elegance. But who will remember these wished wishes? Who will break the codes or tell the stories? I have kept all your letters. I used to imagine your lips along envelopes, your breath on paper. As if you could stay, spelled, between the sheets of rotting books.

When we had filled our bed with old letters and pages torn from books, we had to devise an alternate form. We speak through messages scrawled on scraps: IOUs and grocery lists, please thank you and don't forget to. We become dependent on solitude and shorthand: things stuck on mirrors. A desolate language of custom. Searches for portraits and genealogy end amidst piles of dirty laundry and coffee stains. If all this sounds like resistance, it isn't.

And I want the mad story. Where you say: ask me about chocolate, about curiosity, about the shape and feel of my cock. Ask me about objects in motion and the relative speed of my fucking. Ask me. Where you know when to shut up and I know how to talk so that danger seems reasonable or inevitable. Your breath so close. But every night we climb the stairs, every night we fall asleep with the radio on. In the mornings, sometimes the smell of coffee wakes us even when no one has risen to make it.

You list the words you always misspell. The things I should know before I——. You bring me a little gold fish and say its magic binds us. At midnight, I wait for my fish to vanish into pumpkins. Here no one sleeps. Here no one dreams.

You said stories are at the heart of what explorers and novelists say about the strange world. We are not yet at the stage where we can say *strange* without guilt for what is distant. A postcard of another town lit up with traditional lanterns. Allowing strangers to feed you. Flip the picture: four-poster beds, country walks and afternoon tea. Just for a moment. Let us return to where things stay unchanged like guardians of a magic totality.

You can see this splitting from any distance. The water was a distant memory across the cracked flats, all the dead tipped sideways on the seafloor. Our skin breathes through fog, through the warm clothes where I find the cadence of your voice in the stitching. Say anything, say this tide pool is nothing but our blood. Forget about saving the earth. You collect seawater and I write our names in the sand with a series of broken shells.

This is our best-kept secret. All that is visible across the succession of deep and lost curvatures: Twenty-five blinks. Two eyes. One small hair and the smell of cooking. You have taken all the rice. These days, I sleep very still, as if waiting or counting. *As if* meant something wonderful. We move away from the point of entry. Begin the long unraveling. Breathing is not something we do except in sleep. Return is a word we do not speak.

There is no syntax for loss. There are no words for the loss of words. We cling to what is hard—edges, absolutes, and walls. What remains. So I took things I thought no one would notice: a teacup wrapped in paper, a pocketful of chocolates, a pair of kitchen scissors, a name. A scent that no amount of airing can remove.

After time, our discoveries cease. We have no ancestors, no kin to call. The cabinets grow dusty and collections in jars rot. We long for Egyptian cotton and terra cotta floors, somewhere the dead outnumber the living. We stay up all night and, in the morning, we despise our weakness. We no longer wait, and I have stopped photographing the cliffs. Our breath shrinks (vapor deposition) and winter wind covers the last of the untrammeled places. We are left to carry our own snowfall (cold still).

We begin with surface tension. The measurements made against water. Tell me again about lenses and angles and where the light falls softest. Somewhere between your heart and your cock there's an entire continent. You say this is Film 101: closeups for emotional intensity. Yet I supply the circling movements, clutch the delicate articles of faith: a tesseract to collapse the possible and the not so but who knows. Everything matters. How the camera connects what we cannot: curves to horizons leading to somewhere where aches cease.

We have traveled a long way to this final permutation of comfort. We have crossed the last bridge and submerged the last of the magical realms. I tried to bargain for you—enough for passing, rain for your ghosts. You say visibility fails. And where the trees begin there is no sign of ice, only a strange mix of dark surface and atmosphere. Still we sleep. Still I wake thinking of you. Four or seven times. Looking at your hands, everything becomes possibility. I could almost feel them tense, wrapped around my throat, as we hurtle toward rapture. Slow and winged, like a diminishing point of light.

Our bodies are woven strands to thread irreparable vows. When you take every thing of me that can be in you, you said, then no equivalence, no sound remains. I liked the idea of you in my home, but you were a dream upon waking. Strange verses. The fragments of your songs, *aunque no sea conmigo*. Many years later, after the simple act of survival, I can eat again. Still my body always a tidemark, slowly captive and labored. I bear the marks of your depth-sounding, a flood length of cold.

We paint this house over and over because we are scared. Before it becomes like everywhere else. A strike-slip fault along which we relentlessly crumble. In the wet season, we are islanded in a sea of mud, joining silt and secret. We carry our belongings on our backs, search for cracks before they start to show. You say in some place unknown to us we have practiced the proper ways. In some place, we shared tattoos. There always sinking into want. You say *as it comes* as if arrival could somehow salvage us from the shattering, magnetic earth or deliver us from the flood.

My best move is to leave the room. Before the moon and your hands in your hair. The flashes of imagery: you as the famous actor and me holding the camera. Screen shots of searches. How to Impress an American Girl. Tell her again how your body against her back will hijack entire weeks of her thought. Tell her again of the mornings you wake with her taste even though she is not there. No, we are not the first to cling to infinite life. We are not the first to dream of Shangri-La. But maybe we are the first to stand on the edge and find nothing but 1,887 wrecked miles. Our broken, our wicked, delirious shades.

The magic of the place lies in arriving at the perfect hour. Before the bent and rippled rocks, before the smell of lithosphere and salt. We crack and buckle while the ground lifts and sinks. We arrange the necessary compression. Spit soil in the air. Our center begins to spread, but we are afraid to open our eyes, afraid of what is shifting.

Once you baptized the sun. Once you burnt star-patterns onto cave walls. You gave me a name. We were ruled by ritual and revenge, we tasted the raw honey and gave thanks. We were the people who still took time to find them, all wild animals and face paint and dancing. We didn't know *thrust zone*. We didn't know *ore*. Once we knew the trembling boundaries between lyric and flesh and we were not either.

Do you remember when we were revolutionaries, you said. How room after room filled with the strange sensation that we were flying. Thus knowledge of the sky became essential. How to measure the scattering angle between fires. The diffuse radiation of bodies falling into place. Today we absorb the tremors, shake stillness from the swollen air. You say few places on earth burn but how less wondrous the world would be without them.

And after all the antics of liberation we settled for blank walls and cautious displays. Stuffing and mounting our mildewed artifacts. How many ages passed while we flipped through photos. The barely glimpsable glimpse of our naked bodies was never enough, but we have found our way back to touching ourselves. We have discovered torture. We have discovered the slippery, ravenous chasms, the persistence of summoned want. In those unfulfilled spectacles of concentration: the edge of something grows hard in our mouths, beneath our fingers. Right at the opening, the place on the other side of falling, part dream and part recollection. We were titanium, jacked in, tethered to impulse. You said never has the promise of the future been so beautifully materialized. Better than flying cars or robotic maids. And while this is less beautiful, it is also true: how the clock ticked toward another year while we dismantled the time machines and tore out our eyes when we could no longer behold the dripping wet ache in them.

Because there is more faith there is more blood. We count more stars in the sky yet altitude exhausts us. From time to time we wish that there were not so many points of light, so many wild places. Silence is the glass we look through when we apprehend each other. I have repaired the nets and broken the husks off rice but we have lost our way around *cast* and *mouth*. You say we've arrived where things fall apart and then come back together. You say this looks and feels like what it is—the start of a country or the end of the world.

She remembers his eyes while she sleeps. Pendulous and forging. That unfinished look at the intersection of all the earth's surfaces. Somewhere he dives the great trenches, somewhere he remains faithful. A tectonic prayer against weakening boundaries. But here, where they have converged, there are no dry valleys, no empty seas. She has walked the distance between crust and core and knows the basic strength of rock, the sculpted shapes of erosion. How many of the strange places are even more striking because most people don't know they exist. In her sleep, she conjures those suffocated adagios of islands, against all proof of movement and geometry. She remembers the willing disarmament, the threshing. Tell me again, she says in sleep, who redeems the scarred seabed, the salt wind, the broken devices of navigation? Beneath our once pacific grace, still the burdened rise of bones and flesh. This ruined paradise of breath.

Afterword

This book began in the bedroom. In those dark and half-lit spaces where my parents would read to me at bedtime. Where, as I grew older, I would stay up too late reading books beneath the covers. Where I would scribble stories and poems and hide my journals. For making me a reader by reading to me and surrounding me with books, and for their support and love, I thank my parents: Jeff, Karen, and Nona.

I'm grateful to my teachers who encouraged me as a young reader and writer: Mr. Mike Conlon and Mrs. Sheila Kasprzyk. Any grammatical errors in this book are entirely my fault and in no way reflect your excellent training.

At the University of San Francisco, I was blessed with two years to explore and develop the craft of writing in a rich community of writers. For their wisdom, mentorship, and patience, I thank Aaron Shurin, Elizabeth Robinson, Elizabeth Costello, and Lewis Buzbee. For inspiring me with their words and challenging me to be a better writer, I thank my MFA classmates, especially Jason Buchholz, Joe Cervelin Marina García-Vasquez, Alexandra Mattraw Rosenboom, and Joshua Mohr.

An especially big thanks goes to Jason Buchholz, my fearless Achiote Press partner in crime, for the beautiful chapbook back in the day. But, most importantly, for being a friend and for keeping the Elm Court fridge stocked with beer.

Early drafts of these poems were written as part of (the luminous) Lyn Hejinian's graduate poetry workshop at University of California at Berkeley in 2006. Thanks to all my fellow graduate student writers who helped me escape from my dissertation into poetry. And to Lyn, for her unwavering and enthusiastic support of all my creative endeavors, and for being one of the most authentically compassionate human beings I've had the privilege of knowing—thank you.

In 2006 and 2007, my life changed forever when I signed up for Alfred Arteaga's graduate poetry workshop at UC Berkeley. Because of Alfred, I understand what Tomás Rivera meant when he wrote: *"la voz era la semilla del amor en la oscuridad."* For saying the right words at the right time... for believing in me... this one's for you, AA. You are greatly missed. And *muchas gracias* to my friends and fellow workshoppers: Luis Campos de la Garza, Javier O. Huerta, Augustín Palacios, Alejandro Perez, and Leon Salvatierra.

Many thanks to the folks at Summer Literary Seminars (Kenya, 2006) for the unforgettable experience, and especially to Jodie Hollander: someday we'll drink all the South African white wine again. My life has been enriched by the weeks spent in Mexico City and Oaxaca with Mujeres Poetas en el País de las Nubes. *Muchísimas gracias a Emilio*

Fuego, todos las mujeres poetas, y la gente indígena de Oaxaca por su hospitalidad y generosidad. Un fuerte abrazo a Gabriela Spears-Rico, my homegirl pa' siempre.

Mil gracias to my friend, *el gran poeta* Leon Salvatierra, who said to me: "When you write poetry in English, stay away from fucking r's." Thanks for all the "too p's."

A big, fat Turkish thanks to Daniel Leonard and Michael Subialka for their wicked smart readings and careful feedback in the final stages of this project.

The support of my close friends and family has meant the world to me during the writing of this book. Thanks to my brother, Jonathan, for keeping me in good booze and questionable company over the years. Thanks to my sister, Charlotte, for forgiving me for being a lousy role model. For her graciousness and generosity, I thank Debbie Whaley. Thanks to Jess Stillman for enthusiastically endorsing my bad ideas and for drinking all those margaritas. I owe Joelle Barrios more than I'll ever be able to repay: for the vampires and wine… for the dairy-free desserts… and for being ready to save my life out there on the cliffs of Santorini.

To Kat Sanchez. She knows why.

For all those who've been a part of this journey, thank you for breathing life into these words.

—J.A.R.

JENNIFER A. REIMER grew up in the borderlands of Southern California. Her fiction and poetry have appeared in a number of journals, including: *Our Stories, The Denver Quarterly, The Berkeley Poetry Review, The Chaffey Review, 580 Split, Tinfish, Puerto del Sol, Weave, Zoland*, and *14 Hills*. She has a Ph.D. in Ethnic Studies from the University of California, Berkeley and an MFA in Writing from the University of San Francisco. Currently an assistant professor in the Department of American Culture and Literature at Bilkent University, Jennifer lives and works in Ankara, Turkey. *The Rainy Season Diaries* is her first book. She is the co-editor of Achiote Press (www.achiote press.com).

quale [kwa-lay]: *Eng.* n 1. A property (such as hardness) considered apart from things that have that property. 2. A property that is experienced as distinct from any source it may have in a physical object. *Ital.* pron.a. 1. Which, what. 2. Who. 3. Some. 4. As, just as.

CPSIA information can be obtained at www.ICGtesting.com
Printed in the USA
LVOW08s0642301013

359079LV00004B/92/P